GETTYSBURG

GETTYSBURG

DILLON PRESS
New York

Maxwell Macmillan Canada
Toronto
Maxwell Macmillan International
New York   Oxford   Singapore   Sydney

by Catherine Reef

GF GF DB RRMB

Photo Credits

James Blank: front and back covers
John Reef: pages 2-3, 9, 15, 32, 34, 37, 42, 58 (bottom), 60, and 62;
National Park Service: pages 11, 22, 25, 39, 45, 50, 52, 54; James Blank:
page 58 (top)

Library of Congress Cataloging-in-Publication Data

Reef, Catherine.
    Gettysburg/by Catherine Reef.
       p.   cm. — (Places in American history)
    Includes index.
    Summary: Describes the Battle of Gettysburg, its aftermath, and
the military park that now exists on the battlefield.
    ISBN 0-87518-503-7
    1. Gettysburg (Pa.), Battle of, 1863—Juvenile literature. 2. Lin-
coln, Abraham, 1809-1865. Gettysburg Address—Juvenile litera-
ture. 3. Gettysburg National Military Park (Pa.)—Juvenile litera-
ture. [1. Gettysburg (Pa.), Battle of, 1863. 2. United States—
History—Civil War, 1861-1865—Campaigns. 3. Gettysburg National Military Park (Pa.) 4. National parks and reserves.] I. Title.
II. Series.
E475.53.R34 1992   973.7'349—dc20   91-43653

Dillon Press   Maxwell Macmillan Canada, Inc.
Macmillan Publishing Company 1200 Eglinton Avenue East
866 Third Avenue   Suite 200
New York, NY 10022   Don Mills, Ontario M3C 3N1

Macmillan Publishing Company is part of the Maxwell Communica-
tion Group of Companies.

First edition

Printed in the United States of America
10 9 8 7 6 5 4 3 2 1

★ ★ ★ ★ ★ ★ ★ ★ ★ ★ ★ ★ ★ ★ ★ ★ ★ ★ ★ 13.95

CONTENTS

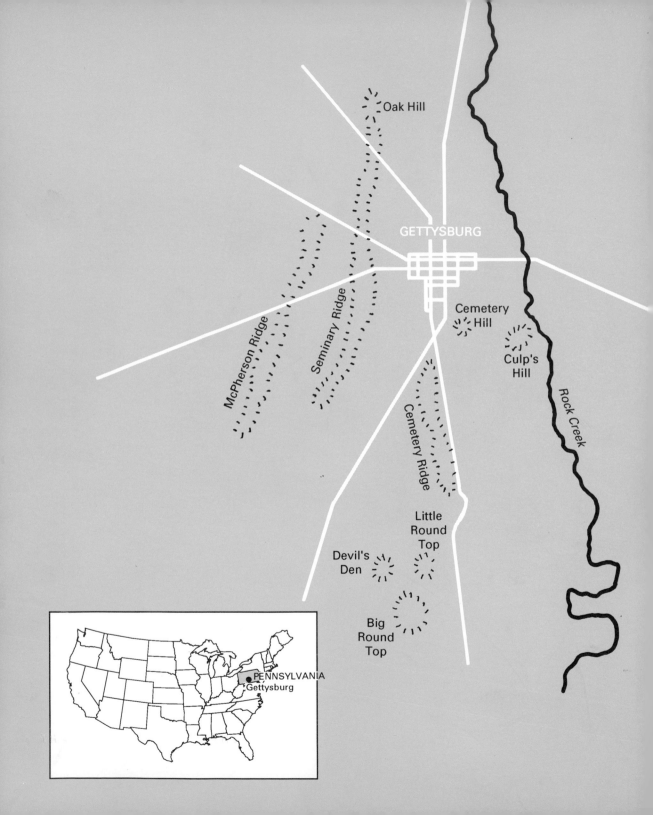

CHAPTER 1

A GREAT
BATTLEFIELD

The noon air was eerily still on that stifling July day in 1863. Soldiers of the Union—the United States of America—crouched behind a stone wall on a slope called Cemetery Hill. Though their heavy, dark-blue uniforms made the soldiers sweat, at least they protected the men from the hot summer sun.

The soldiers looked across a low-lying field where a farmer had tended his crop of wheat just days ago. Now the wheat field had become a battlefield. A house and barn in the valley that had been set on fire still smoldered. Hungry, hot, and tired, the soldiers watched the smoke climb silently skyward.

Beyond the fields lay another ridge and another army. Hidden by trees, soldiers of the Confederate States of America also watched and waited. They came from Virginia, Alabama, Mississippi, and the eight other Southern states that had left the Union to form a nation of their own.

Two years earlier, soldiers on both hilltops had been citizens of the same nation. Now they were enemies in the great Civil War, fighting to decide the future of the American nation. In battles fought with cannons and with guns called rifled muskets, young men had fallen on fields and roadways in many American towns. They had fought in the South: in Manassas Junction, Fredericksburg, and Chancellorsville. They had fought in the North, near Antietam Creek in Maryland. Now the two armies were gathered in the small town of Gettysburg, Pennsylvania, to fight what would be one of the greatest battles of that bloody war.

*Statue of General Winfield Hancock
on Cemetery Hill*

The silence ended at 1:00 P.M. when the boom of a Confederate cannon thundered across the valley. Minutes later the Confederates let loose a storm of cannon fire. Instantly, the blue-clad soldiers on Cemetery Hill dropped to the ground for protection.

One man refused to take cover, however. As cannonballs flew over the soldiers' heads for an hour, General Winfield Hancock fearlessly rode back and forth. A tall man with a thick mustache, Hancock sat up straight on his sleek, black horse, bolstering the courage of the men behind the wall. Soon they would have a chance to fight back, Hancock believed. Soon they would win the great battle.

Some of the soldiers urged Hancock to get down, fearing that he would be killed. But Hancock bravely replied, "There are times when a corps commander's life does not count."

Hancock received a wound in the leg, but he survived the Battle of Gettysburg. Today a

A contemporary photograph showing the Confederate dead at Antietam

statue of Hancock, sitting tall on his fine horse,
stands on Cemetery Hill. It is one of 1,400
monuments and markers that dot the landscape
at Gettysburg National Military Park. These
monuments honor all of the heroic soldiers—
famous and unknown, Union and Confederate—
who took part in that great battle, a battle in
which 51,000 men were killed or wounded or
were missing. It was a battle that became a
turning point in the war. Badly weakened, the
Confederate army was never again to attack on
Union land.

Gettysburg National Military Park is the
most famous memorial to the Civil War. Located
in the rich farmland of southern Pennsylvania,
just a few miles from the Maryland border, it is a
place where cannons line country lanes, where
statues rise from rocks, and where monuments
sprout in wheat fields.

The park's nearly 6,000 acres (2,400 hectares) wrap around the little town of Gettysburg.

The grounds have been maintained carefully so that they look much as they did in 1863 when the two great armies met. But the stone memorials that dot the grounds remind the world that these are not ordinary fields and hills.

Though the Civil War ended in 1865, the events of that war stir strong emotions even today. Many feel sad in remembering the bloodshed that took place in the American countryside. They also feel grateful that the United States healed its wounds and became a strong and powerful nation once again.

Each year, more than one million people travel to Gettysburg to learn about the Civil War and about what happened in that little crossroads town. The exhibits and educational programs in the park's Visitor Center help people understand the great battle and the soldiers' life during the Civil War. The park's plaques and monuments help bring to life the courage and suffering, victory and defeat, that men experienced on the battlefield in those first three days of July in 1863.

But Gettysburg is famous for events that took place after the battle, too. In an effort to show their gratitude and respect for the Union soldiers who died there, the American people created a military cemetery at Gettysburg. And on November 18, 1863, while the graves were still being dug, President Abraham Lincoln traveled to the cemetery. The next day he gave one of the most famous speeches in American history—the Gettysburg Address.

Lincoln's words expressed the sorrow that all Americans felt. He called upon the living to achieve the goal for which these soldiers died: to reunite the divided nation.

Many people who visit Gettysburg today stroll along the paths of the National Cemetery. They gaze at monuments large and small. The tall Soldiers' National Monument seems to stand guard over the Civil War graves. White marble

The memorial to Abraham Lincoln's Gettysburg Address

tombstones mark the graves of Americans who have died in the wars—from the Civil War through the war in Vietnam.

Whatever the war, these men and women fought for the same ideals. They fought for liberty and individual rights. They fought for a strong, free United States of America.

A DIVIDED NATION

Thomas Jefferson sat at a desk in Philadelphia in the early summer of 1776. Hour after hour, his pen scratched out the ideas that formed in his mind. And sentence by sentence, a document took shape. With that document—the Declaration of Independence—the United States of America was born.

This historic document proclaimed that the thirteen British colonies in America were now a new nation, free of English rule. That nation's citizens, it stated, possessed God-given rights—among them, "Life, Liberty, and the pursuit of Happiness"—that could never be taken away.

But the rights that Thomas Jefferson described in the Declaration of Independence did not belong to all Americans. Nearly 700,000 people lived in slavery. They, or their ancestors, had been brought to this country in chains from the far-off coasts of Africa. They worked without pay, and without choice, on the large tobacco farms of the South. They cooked meals, scrubbed floors, and cared for children in the homes of wealthy white Americans.

Thomas Jefferson and other early leaders believed that slavery was a great wrong in the eyes of people and of God. "I tremble for my country when I remember God is just," Jefferson said. Wrote George Washington, "I am principled against this kind of traffic in the human species." But Southern planters depended on their slaves, and the early leaders could only hope that slavery would gradually end.

Instead of dying out, though, the slave trade prospered. In 1793, an American named Eli Whitney invented the cotton gin, a machine that saved growers time and money. The cotton gin removed the tiny seeds from the white fibers of cotton plants, a job that took a long time to do by hand. Soon farmers across the South began planting fields of cotton. People in the industrialized North looked on with dismay as the Southern farmers imported more and more slaves to work on their fields.

As Americans moved west to settle new territories, people disagreed openly about slavery. Congress erupted into angry debates when Missouri and Texas applied to enter the Union as states where slavery was permitted. Representatives from the North argued that slavery was wrong and should not extend into new lands. Those from the South insisted that people in each state had a right to decide about slavery for themselves.

Again and again the North and South compromised—each side gave up some demands to reach an agreement. Missouri was allowed to become a slave state, for example, at the same time that the nation gained a new free state, Maine. But the compromises pleased no one, and people's anger continued to rise.

In 1850, Congress passed the Fugitive Slave Law, giving slave owners the right to pursue and capture runaway slaves. Outraged Northerners responded by forming the Underground Railroad, a secret network of people and hiding places, to help escaped slaves reach freedom in Canada where slavery had been abolished. Harriet Beecher Stowe, the sister of an eloquent preacher and famous abolitionist, Henry Ward Beecher, wrote a book called *Uncle Tom's Cabin*. This best-selling novel described the cruelty of slavery and strengthened the opinions of many Northerners.

A few years later, a fiery man named John Brown, who called himself "a chosen instrument in the hands of God to war against slavery," attracted a group of followers. They rode through Kansas, burning barns and killing people who favored the Southern cause. The United States army captured John Brown in Harpers Ferry, Virginia, after he attacked an armory—a place for storing weapons. The soldiers hanged Brown for his crimes, but he became a hero to many in the North. "John Brown's body lies a-mouldering in the grave," they sang. "His soul goes marching on."

The Republicans, a new political party, called slavery "a great moral, social, and political evil." In 1860, the Republicans nominated Abraham Lincoln for president. This tall, awkward lawyer from Illinois wanted to return to the ideals of Washington, Jefferson, and the other founding fathers. "Slavery," said Lincoln, "was to be restricted and ultimately ended."

More and more, people in the South saw their livelihood and way of life threatened. Some began to declare, "The Union is at an end!" Southern states threatened to secede, or break away, from the United States.

A Mathew Brady photograph of Gettysburg

Lincoln won the presidential election in November: South Carolina seceded in December. By the time Lincoln took the Oath of Office in March of 1861, seven Southern states had seceded and formed a nation of their own, the Confederate States of America.

Some small pockets of land within the Confederate borders still belonged to the United States government. One of these, Fort Sumter, stood beside the harbor at Charleston, South Carolina. On April 14, 1861, Confederate forces aimed guns at Fort Sumter, then fired. For 34 hours, the Confederates bombarded the fort and the Union soldiers inside. At last, cut off from food and other supplies, the Union men surrendered.

With the attack on Fort Sumter, the Civil War began. Even as Lincoln called for volunteers to join the Union army, four more states seceded. The United States was not yet 100 years old, but already its future seemed uncertain. Would the warring states become one nation or two—one slave and one free?

The North, with its factories and greater population, could provide men and weapons for large, well-equipped armies. But those armies lacked experience. More trained soldiers lived in the South, along with a brilliant military leader, General Robert E. Lee. A handsome man with gray hair and a beard, Lee had spent his career in the United States army. He joined the Confederate cause because he could not bear to fight against his home state, Virginia, which had seceded.

In the first two years of the war, the Confederate army seemed equal to the Northern force. A number of the great battles that took place during those years were victories for the South.

Twice the two armies met near a meandering river in the Virginia countryside called Bull Run. Each time, the Confederates sent the Northern forces scrambling back to Washington, D.C.

Confederate General Robert E. Lee

In December of 1862, Confederate gunfire struck down 12,600 Union soldiers as they attacked Lee's army at Fredericksburg, Virginia, beside the Rappahannock River. The Union soldiers appeared to "melt," said one Union officer who survived, "like snow coming down on warm ground." The Southern losses were much lower—only 5,300 men—and many of those had simply gone home for Christmas.

The next May, Lee's Army of Northern Virginia surprised the Union forces at Chancellorsville, a small community not far from Fredericksburg. The Union soldiers had gathered around a lone house in the woods to plan an attack.

Suddenly, the Confederates rushed out of the woods in "a perfect whirlwind of men," one soldier remembered. When the fighting was over, 17,000 Union soldiers lay dead or wounded. The Southerners lost 13,000, but they forced the Union army back across the Rappahannock.

By 1863, the Army of the Potomac had gained one small but important victory against the South. It took place near the small town of Sharpsburg, Maryland. In September of 1862, Lee led 50,000 soldiers into the Union state of Maryland. When they encountered the Union army at Antietam Creek, the greatest day of bloodshed in the war began.

The two armies spent hours fighting in a cornfield and a churchyard. Then the battle moved to a low-lying country road. So many bodies filled this road when the shooting stopped that it gained the nickname "Bloody Lane." Both sides suffered heavy losses, but the North forced Lee's army to return to Virginia.

Another Northern victory seemed possible to the west, where Union general Ulysses S. Grant was trying to take Vicksburg, Mississippi. With the capture of that Southern port city, the North would gain control of the Mississippi River, an important shipping route. It would also weaken the Confederacy by dividing it in two.

Still, Lee's army had won nearly every important battle that it had fought. He had begun to believe it was unbeatable. That spring, Lee devised a new plan—one he hoped would lure Grant away from Vicksburg and, perhaps, cause Lincoln to call for peace. Lee decided to march his army into the North, to steal food and supplies, destroy railroads, and attack cities. He hoped to scare the North into ending the war.

CHAPTER 3

Two Armies Clash

On June 16, Robert E. Lee marched into the Union with 75,000 men. The sight of Confederate soldiers tramping through Maryland and Pennsylvania caused panic in the countryside. The Southerners seized food and land.

Lee had always depended on his cavalry—troops on horseback—to tell him the position of the Union army. But on that day Lee's cavalry was elsewhere, attempting an attack. Lee did not know that the Union army had secretly followed him into Pennsylvania.

The Union army had a new commander, General George Meade, a tall, thin, seasoned soldier. Meade sent out patrols to keep track of the Confederates' location.

Lee had sent a band of soldiers to the small town of Gettysburg. He'd heard it had a supply of shoes, something his army needed badly. Gettysburg was a quiet, hilly place where farmers grew peaches and wheat. It had a population of 2,400 people, a college, and a Lutheran seminary (a school for training ministers). The ten roads that met in Gettysburg carried travelers to large cities and small towns—to places such as Baltimore, Harrisburg, Cashtown, and Emmittsburg.

Early in the morning of July 1, the Southern soldiers came into Gettysburg from the west. They met a Union patrol coming through Gettysburg from the south. The two forces met on a long hill north of town called McPherson Ridge. The Confederates opened fire immediately, shooting again and again.

As the Union soldiers fought back on that hot summer day, both sides sent for help. Some 25,000 Confederates and 19,000 Union soldiers received word of the battle and followed the roads into Gettysburg. The Confederates arrived more quickly, and by midafternoon they pushed the Union army south of town. The Union forces occupied a group of hills in the countryside.

Gettysburg's Evergreen Cemetery was located on one of those hills. A sign in the cemetery warned, "All persons found using firearms in these grounds will be prosecuted with the utmost rigor of the law." The soldiers, with their cannons and muskets, ignored the sign. They swarmed over Cemetery Hill and spread south, in a line that resembled a giant fishhook 3 miles (4.8 kilometers) long. From Cemetery Hill and Culp's Hill, the Union line hooked down along Cemetery Ridge to two large, rocky hills: Little Round Top and Round Top. Standing on the hilltops, Union soldiers could keep watch on Confederate troop movements.

That night, under a full moon, more and

more soldiers arrived. They prepared for the
next day's fighting by the light of their camp-
fires. The confederates lined up in a great curve
6 miles (9.7 kilometers) long, stretching north
and west of the Union line. "I am going to whip
them here, or they are going to whip me," said a
determined Lee.

By sunrise on July 2, 65,000 Confederates
faced 85,000 Union men. It was a day of many
separate fights. Lee wanted to capture the hills,
while Meade was determined to hold them. The
armies battled in a peach orchard, a wheat field,
and a mass of boulders called Devil's Den.

Meade instructed a Union general, Daniel
Sickles, to defend Little Round Top. But on that
hot, clear day, Sickles disobeyed his orders and
left the hilltop undefended. Meade ordered Sick-
les and his men back, but it was too late. The
Confederates had seen their chance to take
Little Round Top and began to charge. The
Southerners hoped to drag their cannons to the

Cemetery Hill

top and attack the Union line.

Another Union general, Gouverneur K. War-ren, climbed to the summit of Little Round Top and saw what was happening. Warren quickly called for soldiers to defend the hill. As the 15th Alabama Regiment, a Southern unit, labored up Little Round Top, four Union regiments raced to the top.

Guns fired on both sides. Five times the Confederates drove the Union soldiers from Little Round Top, but five times the Union gained it back. At day's end, the Union held the strategic hill.

Lee was sure that a massive attack on the third day of battle would succeed. But the day began with two Southern losses. One group of Lee's soldiers attacked Culp's Hill at dawn. After six hours of fighting, the Union forces drove them back. Lee's cavalry finally arrived, but the Union cavalry kept it from reaching the hill.

At noon, the battlefield fell silent. Lee's men

The view from Little Round Top

readied to attack the center of the Union line, on Cemetery Ridge. Lee hoped to divide the Union line in two and then defeat its weakened halves.

At 1:00 P.M., with a sudden, noisy explosion, the Confederates began to fire their cannons at the Northern line. For a while the Union soldiers fought back. But then they stopped shooting to save their bullets and lure the Confederates into the open. They succeeded. Lee thought he had done great damage to the Union line.

Throughout the shooting, 13,000 Confederate soldiers had waited, hidden by trees on a long hill called Seminary Ridge. Many belonged to a division led by General George E. Pickett, and were entering battle for the first time. At 2:00 P.M., Pickett gave his men an order. "Up men and to your posts," he said. "Don't forget that you are from old Virginia."

Soon the historic attack known as Pickett's Charge began. The 13,000 men began to march. Out from the trees they came and crossed a sun-

Cannons sit along Seminary Ridge

drenched wheat field. They headed for a stone wall and a copse, or thicket, of trees on Cemetery Ridge, 1.5 miles (2.4 kilometers) away.

As the Southern soldiers drew near, a Union general ordered his men to fire. Eleven cannons and 1,700 muskets fired at once. Thousands of Confederate soldiers, killed or wounded, fell onto the wheat field. The few who reached the stone wall were killed or captured. The crest of Cemetery Ridge became known as the "high water mark of the Confederacy." It was the closest any Confederates came to taking the Union line.

The fighting lasted an hour, and the Union line held. Of the 13,000 Confederates who marched out of the woods, 6,500 were killed, wounded, or captured. Pickett's Charge had failed. The battle of Gettysburg was over, and the Confederate army had lost.

The three days of fighting had left 51,000 men killed or wounded. The Confederates loaded their wounded into a wagon train 17

Pickett's Charge—as depicted on the
Gettysburg Cyclorama

miles (27.4 kilometers) long and, in the heavy rain of July 4, began the journey home. Its army badly damaged, the South had no more hope of invading the North.

President Lincoln hoped that Meade would follow the Confederates and attack their weakened army before it reached Virginia. This could end the war quickly, he believed. But Meade failed to attack. His men were exhausted, and he had only been in command a few days; he was not sure he would succeed.

Lee and his broken army returned to Virginia. The Civil War raged for nearly two more years, but the South won no more big victories. Lee surrendered to Grant on April 9, 1865, at the village of Appomattox Court House, Virginia, and the Civil War came to an end. It was time for the United States, one nation again, to heal its wounds and look toward the future.

CHAPTER 4

GETTYSBURG REMEMBERS

As the armies left Gettysburg, the town's citizens came out of their homes. They found their fences broken and riddled with bullet holes. Their wheat lay trampled. Discarded, broken weapons littered the landscape. More than 6,000 bodies lay scattered across the fields and hills. Thousands of wounded men remained, too injured to travel. The people of Gettysburg brought the wounded into their homes and cared for them as well as they could. Still, many died every day.

Some citizens helped the Union soldiers as they buried their dead. They buried the bodies throughout the fields in shallow graves and trenches. When a dead soldier could be identi-

fied, citizens penciled his name on a wooden marker beside the grave site.

The governor of Pennsylvania, Andrew Curtin, visited Gettysburg shortly after the battle. The many scattered graves troubled him greatly. He asked a Gettysburg attorney, David Wills, to find land for a cemetery to hold the Union dead. Wills chose a piece of land on the northern slope of Cemetery Hill, next to the Evergreen Cemetery.

While the nation was still at war, people in the North lacked concern for the dead Confederate soldiers. They were still considered to be the enemy. It wasn't until after the war that civic organizations from the South removed the Confederate dead from Gettysburg and reburied them in southern cities.

A landscape architect named William Saunders created a design for the 17 acres (6.9 hectares) that were to hold the bodies of 3,500 Union soldiers. According to his plan, the dead

Union soldiers lie buried in Gettysburg's graves

from each state would be buried together. The graves would form a semicircle around a tall monument.

Moving the bodies to the new cemetery took months. The wooden markers with penciled names helped the workers identify many bodies. But 1,664 could still not be identified and were buried as unknowns.

The cemetery's planners decided to hold a dedication ceremony before the burials were completed. They invited Edward Everett, the president of Harvard University, to speak on the occasion. Everett had a reputation for giving stirring, patriotic speeches. The planners sent an invitation to President Lincoln, but did not expect him to attend. When Lincoln did accept the invitation, he, too, was asked to speak at the ceremony.

Fifteen thousand people gathered at Gettysburg's new military cemetery on November 19, 1863. Shortly after noon, Everett stood

An artist depticts Lincoln delivering his Gettysburg Address

before the crowd. One observer recalled that he "stood a moment in silence, regarding the battle-field and the distant beauty of the South Mountain range." Then Everett spoke, for nearly two hours. He spoke of the burial customs in ancient Greece and the reasons nations go to war. He described the Battle of Gettysburg in detail and praised the soldiers who died there.

The audience sang a hymn, and then Lincoln rose to speak. He talked for only two minutes, but his Gettysburg Address became one of the best-known speeches in American history. Lincoln reminded the crowd that their country's founders had created a nation "conceived in Liberty, and dedicated to the proposition that all men are created equal." The soldiers buried in the new cemetery, the president said, gave their lives to preserve that nation. He asked the living to continue this task, so that "this nation, under God, shall have a new birth of freedom—and that government of the people, by the people, for the people, shall not perish from the earth."

Later, as the cemetery took shape, another Gettysburg attorney, David McConaughy, noted that the battlefield had historic importance, too. Like Mount Vernon—George Washington's home in Virginia—it should be preserved, he proposed. That way, Americans could learn about the battle by visiting the site.

McConaughy explained his idea to the town's business leaders. He suggested that the civic leaders buy and preserve as much of the battlefield as possible.

McConaughy's fellow citizens called his idea "a happy and patriotic conception." They formed an organization, the Gettysburg Battlefield Memorial Association, to buy the land, construct roads, and build monuments. They invited all Americans to contribute ten dollars to join the association.

By 1888, 25 years after the Battle of

Gettysburg, the association had acquired almost 500 acres (202 hectares) along the Union line. Workers had built 13 miles (20.9 kilometers) of roads and placed more than 200 signs and memorials on the battlefield. These marked the sites of events with historic importance for the Union. Many Northerners remained angry at the South for years following the Civil War. The association had no interest in honoring the Confederates at Gettysburg.

In the years ahead, some people called for the federal government to take over the battlefield. Without federal control, they believed, the battlefield would become too commercial and lose its historic character. Already some business people were building an electric railway to take tourists to the battle sites.

The United States War Department acquired the battlefield in 1895. The government decided to preserve the entire history of the battle, not just the Union side. Surveyors measured out both Union and Confederate lines. The government directed that statues and memorials explain the history of both sides, "without praise or censure." The United States Supreme Court decided that the electric railway could not remain on the site.

Using photographs from 1863 and maps made by General Gouverneur K. Warren as guides, laborers replanted forests that had since been cleared for farmland. They cleared fields that had once been open and were now overgrown. The workers took many Civil War cannons out of storage and placed them along the battle lines at Gettysburg. Some of these cannons had been used in the battle itself.

The year 1913 marked the 50th anniversary of the battle. That summer, 55,000 Union and Confederate veterans of the battle reunited at Gettysburg. They relived their wartime memories as they strolled on the battlefield looking at the monuments. On July 3, 150 former Confed-

erates reenacted Pickett's Charge. Old Union soldiers met them on Cemetery Ridge with handshakes instead of bullets.

In 1933 the National Park Service took over responsibility for the battlefield. Now called the Gettysburg National Military Park, the site covered 2,116 acres (857 hectares) of park land, with 900 monuments and 415 cannons.

Two thousand veterans walked the battle-field in 1938, the 75th anniversary of the battle. Most of the men were more than 90 years old; some were more than 100. On the evening of July 3, they gathered at the dedication of the Eternal Light Peace Memorial. President Franklin D. Roosevelt looked on as two aged veterans removed the American flag that cov-ered the tall stone structure. A flame on the monument would burn without ceasing. It would be a beacon of hope for a peaceful future.

By the time 30,000 people gathered in Gettysburg in 1963, however, Americans had

In 1913, three Union soldiers gathered to recollect their Gettysburg experience.

PEACE ETERNAL IN A NAT

fought World War II and the Korean War. American military forces were in the Southeast Asian nation of Vietnam. It was the 100th anniversary of the battle of Gettysburg as former president Dwight D. Eisenhower addressed the crowd. He reminded those present that the Civil War had been fought to bring equality to all Americans. That goal had not yet been achieved, Eisenhower said. Many black Americans still faced discrimination.

As the years pass, America continues to observe the anniversary of the Battle of Gettysburg. One of the most significant activities of the 1988 125th anniversary was the rededication of the Eternal Light Peace Memorial. This ceremony helped to deepen the reconciliation on the field fostered by earlier reunions. Also in 1988 the National Park Service sponsored "living history encampments," so that visitors could see how Civil War soldiers lived. Volunteers in uniforms performed military drills

Veterans dedicated the Eternal Light Peace Memorial in 1938

and demonstrated activities of soldiers' daily lives. When they were not fighting or marching, the soldiers lived in tents, boiling coffee over open fires.

The experience dramatized the human side of the Civil War. It showed many visitors that the soldiers at Gettysburg were ordinary Americans with families and dreams much like their own.

In 1988 people reenacted Pickett's Charge

CHAPTER 5

A VISIT TO GETTYSBURG

Ten roads carry people to Gettysburg today, just as they did in 1863. They carry people from Baltimore, Harrisburg, and even the small town of Emmittsburg. But they also bring visitors from places throughout the world.

More than one million people come to the Gettysburg National Military Park each year. As they stand beneath the trees on Gettysburg's hilltops, they can imagine that the fields before them are filled with fighting men.

The park's large brick Visitor Center is the first stop for most tourists. The exhibits there help them understand what it was like to be a soldier in the Civil War. On display are the uniforms of Union and Confederate soldiers. Blue for the Union and brownish-gray for the Confederacy, they were made of heavy cloth that was hot and uncomfortable under the summer sun. Hundreds of muskets and pistols fill long, glass cases; the Visitors Center holds one of the world's largest collections of Civil War firearms.

The Center's Electric Map helps people understand what they will see on the battlefield. Seated in a darkened theater, visitors watch as colored lights on the 750-square-foot (67.5-square-meter) map show the movement of troops in Gettysburg. A recorded voice narrates the battle's events, helping the audience follow the movements of troops around Gettysburg.

A separate building houses the Gettysburg Cyclorama. In 1881, a French artist named Paul Philippoteaux traveled to the United States. He wanted to paint a picture that would make people feel as if they were in the midst of the action at Gettysburg. He spoke with people who witnessed Pickett's Charge. He sketched and

later painted the battlefield landscape.

Philippoteaux's circular painting, the Cyclorama, surrounds viewers with scenes of war. Soldiers clash in wheat fields. Wounded men fall from their horses. In a ramshackle hospital, a doctor prepares to remove a soldier's injured leg. Viewers can easily imagine themselves at the top of Cemetery Ridge on July 3, 1863.

Many people who tour the battlefield stop at the Eternal Light Peace Memorial. The lettering across the monument's base expresses its purpose—the hope for "Peace Eternal in a Nation United." When the memorial was dedicated in 1938, people hoped that its flame would burn without stopping. But during the 1970s, Americans grew concerned about saving energy. The eternal flame burned natural gas, and fearing that it wasted fuel, government workers put it out in 1974. The eternal flame began to burn again in 1978, powered by energy-saving electric lights.

On Seminary Ridge, the people of the

Above: the building that houses the Cyclorama
Below: a section of Philippoteaux's Cyclorama

Southern states placed monuments to their soldiers who fought at Gettysburg. The large North Carolina Memorial catches many eyes. It depicts a group of Confederate soldiers moving toward the Union line. One soldier proudly holds the Confederate flag high in the air while another crouches low, pointing the way. The others scan the horizon, alert for danger and ready to fire their muskets.

Just a short distance away stands the Virginia Memorial. At the top of a broad stone pillar, a statue of Robert E. Lee seems to be looking across the field. Lee appears hopeful as he sits upon his horse, Traveller.

On Little Round Top, a statue of Gouverneur K. Warren, the "Savior of Little Round Top," surveys the scene of his victory. The statue stands on one of the boulders that protected the Union soldiers from Confederate gunfire as they fought for control of the hill. This rocky hilltop is a favorite spot for viewers today, because it

The Eternal Light Peace Memorial

VIRGINIA TO HER SONS AT GETTYSBURG

offers a sweeping view of Gettysburg's hills and valleys.

Just as the Confederate line contains memorials to soldiers from the Southern states, the Union line is the site of monuments to the Northern forces. The largest monument on the battlefield is the Pennsylvania Memorial, rising 110 feet (33 meters) into the air. Many soldiers from Pennsylvania fought at Gettysburg, and bronze plaques at the memorial's base contain the names of more than 34,000. At the top of the memorial's domed roof, the figure of an angel—representing victory and peace—raises a sword into the air.

One of Gettysburg's monuments is not made of metal or stone. The copse of trees toward which Pickett's soldiers marched stands as a living memorial on Cemetery Ridge. This spot is the "high water mark"—the farthest advance of the Confederate soldiers. It marks the end of the battle and a turning point in the Civil War.

Above: one of many memorials placed by states, the North Carolina Memorial is particularly striking
Below: the Virginia Memorial

Beside the copse of trees, a bronze statue of an open book honors the troops who fought on Cemetery Ridge. In a spirit of healing, the book's pages list both Union and Confederate forces.

Gettysburg is famous for the battle that occurred there. It is also remembered for the events that followed. In the National Cemetery, among ancient trees with gnarled, thick trunks, stands a monument to Lincoln's Gettysburg Address. In the world's only memorial to a speech, a statue of Lincoln rests between plaques containing his deeply felt words.

Another monument stands on the spot where Lincoln gave that historic speech. Around the Soldier's National Monument, the graves of the Union dead fan out in a semicircle. From the top of the tall, stone structure, a robed figure watches over them. She represents liberty, an ideal for which these men fought and died.

Four more carved figures surround the

monument's base. One of the figures stands for war. Two represent peace and plenty—dreams the soldiers held for after the war. The fourth figure represents history. The men who died at Gettysburg sacrificed their dreams, but they earned a place in their nation's history. Even those who died unknown are remembered in spirit if not name by millions today.

GETTYSBURG:
A HISTORICAL TIME LINE

1860   Abraham Lincoln is elected president. Southern states begin to secede from the United States.

1861   The Confederates attack Fort Sumter; the Civil War begins.

1863   General Robert E. Lee's Confederate army crosses the Potomac River and enters Union territory. On July 1, Lee's soldiers encounter Union forces at Gettysburg, Pennsylvania. For three days, the Union and Confederate armies fight the greatest battle of the Civil War. The Confederate army is defeated and retreats across the Potomac. Attorney David Wills acquires 17 acres of land on Cemetery Hill for a military cemetery. On November 19, the new cemetery is dedicated, and President Abraham Lincoln gives his Gettysburg Address.

1864   The Gettysburg Battlefield Memorial Association is formed.

1865   The Civil War ends.

1881   French artist Paul Philippoteaux travels to Gettysburg to do research for his massive circular painting of Pickett's Charge.

1895   The United States War Department acquires the Gettysburg battlefield.

1913   The 50th anniversary of the Battle of Gettysburg. Union and Confederate veterans gather in Gettysburg and reenact Pickett's Charge.

1933   Management of the battlefield is turned over to the National Park Service.

1938   The 75th anniversary of the Battle of Gettysburg. Two thousand Union and Confederate veterans gather at Gettysburg. The Eternal Light Peace Memorial is dedicated.

1963   The 100th anniversary of the Battle of

Gettysburg. Volunteers reenact Pickett's Charge.

1972   The United States government acquires the title to the military cemetery.

1988   The 125th anniversary of the Battle of Gettysburg. Volunteers present living history encampments. The Eternal Light Peace Memorial is rededicated.

Visitor Information

Hours

The Gettysburg National Military Park is open every day of the year except Thanksgiving, Christmas, and New Year's Day. The Visitor Center is open from 8:00 A.M. to 5:00 P.M., and the Cyclorama is open from 9:00 A.M. to 5:00 P.M. Tour roads within the park are open from 6:00 A.M. until 10:00 P.M.

Admission

Admission to the park and Visitor Center is free. For those age 16 and over, there are separate admission charges for the Electric Map and the Cyclorama.

Tours

Brochures are available for a self-guided automobile tour of the park as well as for self-guided walks. Visitors may hire a guide to conduct a two-hour tour of the park in their automobile. Park rangers lead walking tours and other activities regularly, at no extra charge.

Special Events

A Memorial Day Ceremony is held in the National Cemetery on the last Monday in May.

The anniversary of the Battle of Gettysburg (July 1-July 3) is observed with demonstrations of Civil War drills and the daily activities of soldiers. Dedication Day is held November 19 to commemorate Lincoln's Gettysburg Address. A guest speaker addresses visitors in the National Cemetery on this day.

For more information, contact:

Gettysburg National Military Park
Gettysburg, PA 17325
(717) 334-1124

The Gettysburg Travel Council
35 Carlisle Street
Gettysburg, PA 17325
(717) 334-6274

Index